"Your whole life is a manifestation of the thoughts that go on in your head."

Lisa Nichols

Table of Contents

Introduction

How Your Brain Learned to Lie to You

If you've been in business for more than five minutes, you've probably heard some version of: *"Women entrepreneurs are resilient… resourceful… inspiring."*

Which is often code for: *"We're amazed you're pulling this off with almost no support, unclear expectations, and a voice in your head that never shuts up."*

Women business owners are building companies, creating jobs, and driving economic growth across the world, often while carrying far more invisible weight than anyone sees.

But the most exhausting part of that weight isn't always external. It's internal. Most of us have a voice in our head that talks nonstop all day, every day. Sometimes it narrates. Sometimes it critiques. Sometimes it replays conversations that already happened or invents conversations that never will. This is what is called mental chatter - the constant internal dialogue that shapes how we interpret the world, ourselves, and our own capability.

If you read my book "Master Your Mindset: How Women Step Up," you know that mental chatter isn't intuition. It isn't wisdom. And it definitely isn't always telling the truth. In fact, much of what that voice says is simply a recording.

Your brain is a pattern-recognition machine. It absorbs messages from parents, spouses, teachers, bosses, culture, past relationships, and society at large, then repeats them back to you on a loop. Over time, repetition turns suggestion into belief. Belief turns into identity. And identity quietly dictates how big you're willing to play.

That's how smart, capable women end up doubting themselves without realizing why. Your brain says things like:

- *"You should probably wait until you're more prepared."*
- *"Don't raise your prices yet."*
- *"Who do you think you are to want more?"*
- *"You should be able to handle this on your own."*

And because the voice sounds like *you*, you assume it must be right.

But here's the critical truth: mental chatter is not objective, it's conditioned. Over time, it evolves into something even more powerful, and more limiting. It hardens into what is called mental lies: beliefs that feel factual but are actually inherited, outdated, and misaligned with who you are now.

This is where mindset malware sets in. Just like a computer virus runs quietly in the background, these lies operate beneath conscious awareness. They don't scream. They whisper. And they don't stop you outright, they slow you down, shrink your decisions, and cap your ambition just enough to feel "reasonable."

Nothing limits the growth of a woman-owned business faster than a brain running on old code. Not lack of intelligence. Not lack of work ethic. Not lack of vision. The real bottleneck is believing thoughts that were never designed to support your success.

This book is about identifying the seven most common lies women entrepreneurs internalize and dismantling them. Not through hustle or positive thinking, but through awareness, reframing, and leadership-level truth.

Because when you change the conversation happening in your head, you don't just feel better.

- You lead differently.
- You price differently.
- You decide faster.
- You scale smarter.
- You stop shrinking.

And that's when everything changes.

At the end of each chapter, I'm going to offer you three possible ways to reframe that lie to be empowering. Not every reframe will land the same way for every person, and that is intentional. A reframe is not an affirmation you are supposed to force yourself to believe. It is a bridge between an old belief and a more useful one. Some reframes will feel immediately true. Others may feel aspirational, uncomfortable, or even slightly irritating. Pay attention to that reaction.

The reframe that works best for you is the one your brain is willing to engage with, even if it does not feel fully natural yet. If a statement feels so far from your current reality that your mind rejects it outright, set it aside for now. Choose the reframe that feels believable enough to practice, repeat, and test in real decisions. Over time, what once felt like a stretch often becomes your new default. Reframing is not about positive thinking. It is about choosing a thought that gives you more options, more agency, and more room to lead.

When mental chatter runs unchecked, it doesn't just create noise, it starts to write rules. Over time, those repeated thoughts harden into beliefs about what's possible, what's appropriate, and what you're "ready" for.

That's where the lies take hold. And the very first one usually sounds responsible, rational, even humble. It tells you to wait. To prepare more. To prove yourself just a little longer before you step fully into your authority.

That lie is so common, so socially reinforced, that most women don't even realize they're operating under it. Which is exactly why it's the first one we're going to dismantle.

Lie #1: You Need to be Twice as Qualified to be Taken Seriously

This lie rarely shows up announcing itself. It does not say, "You are not good enough." That would be too easy to spot. Instead, it dresses itself up as responsibility.

It sounds like:

- "I just need one more certification."
- "I should probably wait until I have more experience."
- "I want to be fully prepared before I step into that role."
- "Once I feel more confident, then I will go for it."

On the surface, these thoughts sound reasonable. Mature, even. After all, who would argue against being prepared?

The problem is that this lie has no finish line. For many women entrepreneurs, preparation becomes a holding pattern. The bar for readiness keeps moving just out of reach, not because more skill is required, but because the brain has learned to equate caution with safety. Over time, "being responsible" quietly turns into delaying decisions, downplaying expertise, and waiting for permission that never comes.

Meanwhile, less qualified people with louder confidence move forward without hesitation. This is not because they are more capable. It is because they have not been conditioned to believe they must earn the right to speak, lead, or charge at a higher level.

Women are often taught that competence must be proven before authority is claimed. That message starts early and shows up everywhere, in classrooms, workplaces, media, and leadership models that reward certainty over substance.

By the time a woman starts her own business, that conditioning has often become internalized. The voice in her head says, "You are good, but not quite ready yet."

The truth is that confidence does not arrive after mastery. It is built through action.

No amount of additional preparation will silence mental chatter if the underlying belief remains that you are not allowed to step forward until you feel perfectly qualified. That feeling rarely arrives on its own. It is created by choosing to move anyway.

Here is the truth that changes everything: You do not need to be twice as qualified. You need to be clear. Clear about the value you provide. Clear about the problems you solve. Clear about the outcomes you create for clients.

Clarity builds credibility faster than credentials ever will.

This does not mean skill and experience do not matter. They do. But they are not the gatekeepers to leadership. When you speak from lived experience, grounded expertise, and results you have already delivered, you are not asking for permission. You are claiming your lane.

The real cost of believing this lie is not missed opportunities. It is the slow erosion of self-trust. Every time you tell yourself to wait, to prepare more, to hold back, you reinforce the idea that you cannot be trusted with the next level yet. Over time, that belief shapes how you price, how you position yourself, and how big you allow your business to become.

Leading bigger starts with a simple but radical shift. You stop asking whether you are qualified enough and start asking whether you are willing to lead from where you are.

Because readiness is not something you earn in private. It is something you build in motion. Once you stop waiting for permission to lead, another lie tends to surface almost immediately. It shows up the moment you put a number on your work. The moment you send a proposal. The moment you consider raising your rates or charging in a way that reflects the real value you deliver.

This lie does not question your competence. It questions your right to be paid well for it. And for many women entrepreneurs, it is one of the most financially damaging beliefs they carry.

~~~~~~~~~~~~~~~~~~~~~
~~~~~~~~~~~~~~~~~~~~~

Choose Your Reframe

Even when you recognize a thought as a lie, it can be surprisingly hard to stop listening to it. Awareness alone is rarely enough. When your brain is under pressure, it will default to familiar patterns unless you give it something more useful to reach for. Creating an empowering reframe gives you an intentional response to use when the old narrative shows up.

Below are several possible reframes. Choose the one that feels most believable and supportive to practice the next time this lie appears. If it stops working, choose a different one.

- **Option A:** I do not need to feel ready to lead. I need to be willing to lead from where I am.
- **Option B:** Clarity and experience create credibility faster than waiting for confidence ever will.
- **Option C:** I am already qualified to take the next step. Readiness is built in motion, not in hiding.

One Action to Take

Identify one opportunity you have been postponing because you feel "not ready enough" and take a visible step toward it this week. That might mean raising your hand, submitting the proposal, having the conversation, or making the decision without waiting for additional validation.

Reflection Questions to Journal About:

1. Where in your business are you waiting to feel more ready before taking action?
2. What evidence already exists that you are qualified for the next level you are considering?
3. What decision would you make this month if you trusted your current expertise?
4. How has over-preparing protected you, and how has it limited you?

Lie #2: Charging What You're Worth Will Scare Clients Away

This lie has excellent timing. It appears just as your business starts to gain traction. Just as demand increases. Just as your calendar fills and your capacity tightens. Instead of celebrating that growth, your brain offers a warning disguised as concern.

It says:

- People will not pay that.
- You should keep your prices accessible.
- What if they say no?
- You do not want to seem greedy.

At first glance, this sounds like empathy. Consideration. Professionalism. In reality, it is fear wearing a friendly outfit.

Many women entrepreneurs have been conditioned to associate likability with affordability. To believe that being kind means being flexible. That being grateful means not asking for too much. Over time, that conditioning turns pricing into an emotional decision rather than a strategic one.

So women undercharge. They overdeliver. They customize endlessly. They say yes when they should say no. And then they wonder why they are exhausted, resentful, or stuck below the revenue level they know they are capable of reaching.

Here is the truth most women are never taught: Your pricing is not a referendum on your worth as a human being. It is a business decision based on value, outcomes, and capacity. When you price too low, you do not become more generous. You become less sustainable.

Clients who are a strong fit are not scared away by confident pricing. They are reassured by it. Clear pricing signals clarity of thinking, professionalism, and trust in the results you deliver. It tells the market that you understand the value of your work and expect it to be taken seriously.

The clients who disappear when you raise your rates are not a loss. They are information. They are telling you that the relationship only worked when you were overextending yourself.

One of the most common mistakes women entrepreneurs make is tying pricing to effort rather than impact. They think about hours worked, energy spent, and how hard something feels. Clients, on the other hand, care about outcomes. They care about problems solved, time saved, revenue gained, and stress reduced.

When you shift your pricing from effort-based to value-based, something important happens. You stop apologizing. You stop explaining. You stop negotiating against yourself before anyone else has even spoken. And yes, some people will say no. That is not failure. That is filtering.

A business that is designed to scale cannot be built on universal approval. It must be built on alignment. The right clients do not need convincing. They need clarity.

The deeper cost of believing this lie is not just financial. It is energetic. Underpricing teaches your brain that your work is negotiable. Over time, that belief bleeds into how you show up, how you market, and how you lead. You begin to shrink preemptively, just in case someone might be uncomfortable.

Charging appropriately is not about ego. It is about integrity. It is about matching your pricing to the value you deliver, the capacity you have, and the business you are building next, not the one you are trying to outgrow.

You do not scare away the right clients by charging well. You invite them in. Once you stop waiting to lead and stop underpricing your work, another belief tends to rush in to fill the space. It reframes growth as endurance. It suggests that success is something you earn through exhaustion. This lie does not question your ambition. It exploits it. And it convinces far too many women that constant effort is the price of legitimacy.

~~~~~~~~~~~~~~~~~

Choose Your Reframe

Even when you recognize a thought as a lie, it can be surprisingly hard to stop listening to it. Awareness alone is rarely enough. When your brain is under pressure, it will
~~~~~~~~~~~~~~~~~

default to familiar patterns unless you give it something more useful to reach for. Creating an empowering reframe gives you an intentional response to use when the old narrative shows up.

Below are several possible reframes for this lie. Choose the one that feels most believable and supportive to practice the next time this lie appears. If it stops working, choose a different one.

- **Option A:** My pricing reflects the value and outcomes I deliver, not my need to be liked.
- **Option B:** The right clients are reassured by clear, confident pricing.
- **Option C:** Sustainable pricing allows me to show up as a better leader, not a resentful one.

One Action to Take

Choose one offering and adjust the pricing to better reflect its value, scope, or impact. Communicate the price clearly and confidently, without over-explaining or apologizing. Pay attention to how this changes both client response and your own energy.

Reflection Questions to Journal About

1. How do you currently decide what to charge, and what
    emotions show up around pricing?
2. Where might you be pricing based on effort rather than
    impact or outcomes?
3. What would change in your business if your pricing
    reflected sustainability rather than likability?
4. Which clients or opportunities are you trying to protect
    yourself from losing, and why?

Lie #3: If You Were a Real Entrepreneur, You'd Hustle 24x7

This lie is deeply embedded in modern business culture. It glorifies long hours, celebrates burnout as commitment, and treats rest as something you earn only after you have proven yourself. For women entrepreneurs, it often carries an additional layer of pressure. You are not just expected to work hard. You are expected to make it look effortless.

So you push. You power through. You answer emails late at night. You tell yourself this is just a season. Then that season never ends.

Hustle culture teaches that the more hours you work, the more legitimate your success will be. But in reality, hours worked and business growth are not directly correlated. Many women discover this the hard way. They work harder than ever and still hit a plateau.

The reason is simple: a business that relies entirely on your personal effort is not a scalable business. It is a job with good branding.

Early-stage hustle can feel necessary. You are building, learning, and testing. But when hustle becomes your primary strategy, it quietly caps your growth. There are only so many hours in a day, and eventually, your capacity becomes the bottleneck.

This is where many women get stuck. They believe stepping back means losing control. They believe rest signals laziness. They believe delegation is something they will do later, when things calm down.

But things do not calm down on their own. Sustainable growth comes from systems, not stamina. Entrepreneurs who scale successfully do not work harder forever. They change how the work gets done. They invest in processes, delegation, automation, and decision frameworks that reduce cognitive load and free up leadership capacity.

This is not about doing less because you care less. It is about doing less of the wrong work so you can do more of the right work.

Hustle culture also erodes judgment. Chronic exhaustion narrows perspective, slows decision-making, and increases reactivity. When you are tired, everything feels urgent and nothing feels strategic. Over time, that state becomes normalized, and you forget what clear thinking even feels like.

Rest is not a reward. It is infrastructure. When you protect your energy, you protect your ability to lead. When you build white space into your schedule, you create room for insight, creativity, and better decisions. Those are not luxuries. They are leadership tools.

Letting go of this lie requires a shift in identity. You stop measuring your value by how much you endure. You stop proving your commitment through self-sacrifice. You start designing a business that works without breaking you.

Real entrepreneurship is not about running yourself into the ground. It is about building something that can stand without you holding it up every second.

As soon as you stop equating leadership with exhaustion, another lie tends to surface. This one is quieter, more subtle, and often delivered as "helpful feedback." It is less about how hard you work and more about how much of

yourself you are allowed to show while doing it. This lie
does not ask you to work less. It asks you to be less.

~~~~~~~~~~~~~~~~~~

Choose Your Reframe

Even when you recognize a thought as a lie, it can be
surprisingly hard to stop listening to it. Awareness alone is
rarely enough. When your brain is under pressure, it will
default to familiar patterns unless you give it something
more useful to reach for. Creating an empowering reframe
gives you an intentional response to use when the old
narrative shows up.

Below are several possible reframes for this lie. Choose the
one that feels most believable and supportive to practice
the next time this lie appears. If it stops working, choose a
different one.

- **Option A:** My job is to build systems, not to exhaust
  myself.
- **Option B:** Rest and white space improve my judgment
  and leadership.
~~~~~~~~~~~~~~~~~~

- **Option C:** Working harder is not the same as leading smarter.

One Action to Take

Identify one recurring task or decision that drains your time or attention and either delegate it, systematize it, or remove it entirely. Use the reclaimed time for thinking, planning, or rest, not more busywork.

Reflection Questions to Journal About

1. What parts of your business currently rely too heavily on your personal effort?
2. Where are you using exhaustion as a substitute for systems or structure?
3. How does chronic busyness affect the quality of your decisions and leadership?
4. What is one boundary or system you could implement to protect your energy this quarter?

Lie #4: You Need to Tone it Down

This lie almost never comes straight out and says what it means. Instead, it shows up as suggestion. It sounds like:

- You are a lot.
- You might want to soften your message.
- Try not to come across as too intense.
- You should be careful how that lands.

Sometimes it is said out loud. More often, it is implied. And over time, it becomes internalized.

Women entrepreneurs learn quickly that visibility comes with consequences. The more confident you are, the more likely you are to be labeled intimidating. The more decisive you are, the more likely you are to be seen as abrasive. The more ambitious you are, the more pressure you feel to explain yourself.

So you edit. You soften language. You second-guess tone. You add disclaimers. You make yourself easier to consume. But the truth is that none of this makes you a better leader. It makes you smaller.

This lie is especially damaging because it is socially reinforced. Women are praised for being collaborative, agreeable, and accommodating. Those traits are not inherently bad. The problem arises when they become requirements for acceptance.

Leadership does not require shrinking to make others comfortable. When women tone themselves down, they do not become more effective. They become less visible. Their ideas lose edge. Their authority blurs. Their message weakens. And slowly, they begin to confuse being liked with being respected.

Here is the truth this lie obscures: Your ambition is not a character flaw. Your confidence is not arrogance. Your clarity is not aggression.

What some people experience as "too much" is often simply a woman refusing to minimize herself. There will always be people who are uncomfortable with a woman who speaks plainly, leads decisively, and owns her expertise without apology. That discomfort is not a signal to retreat. It is a signal that you are operating outside outdated expectations.

Toning yourself down does not protect you. It trains others how to treat you. When you consistently soften your presence to avoid friction, you teach people to expect less from you. You also teach yourself that your natural leadership style is something to manage rather than trust.

Strong leadership requires congruence. When who you are internally does not match how you show up externally, it creates friction inside you first. That friction drains energy, confidence, and clarity. Over time, it becomes harder to lead at full capacity because you are constantly monitoring yourself instead of focusing on impact.

The reframe here is simple, but not always easy. You do not need to be louder. You do not need to be harsher. You do not need to change who you are. You need to stop editing yourself to fit rooms that were not designed with you in mind.

Leadership is not about being palatable. It is about being effective. And effectiveness does not require you to tone it down. It requires you to show up fully.

Once you stop shrinking your presence, another belief often surfaces, one that feels less personal and more structural. It whispers that there is only so far a woman-owned business can realistically go. That growth beyond a certain point is rare, risky, or reserved for someone else. This lie does not question your talent. It questions your trajectory.

~~~~~~~~~~~~~~~~~

Choose Your Reframe

Even when you recognize a thought as a lie, it can be surprisingly hard to stop listening to it. Awareness alone is rarely enough. When your brain is under pressure, it will default to familiar patterns unless you give it something more useful to reach for. Creating an empowering reframe gives you an intentional response to use when the old narrative shows up.
~~~~~~~~~~~~~~~~~

Below are several possible reframes for this lie. Choose the one that feels most believable and supportive to practice the next time this lie appears. If it stops working, choose a different one.

- **Option A:** My clarity is not aggression. My ambition is not a flaw.
- **Option B:** I do not need to edit myself to be effective.
- **Option C:** Leadership requires presence, not palatability.

One Action to Take

In your next leadership moment, speak or act without softening your message. Share the idea, set the boundary, or make the decision clearly and directly. Notice what happens when you do not preemptively shrink.

Reflection Questions to Journal About

1. Where do you find yourself editing, softening, or holding back in your leadership or messaging?
2. What reactions are you trying to avoid by doing so?
3. How would your leadership change if you allowed yourself to be fully visible and clear?

4. What is one situation where you can practice showing up without self-editing?

Lie #5: Women-Led Businesses Can Only Grow So Big

This lie tends to show up right as momentum builds. You are doing well. Revenue is growing. Demand is steady. And yet, a quiet narrative begins to circulate, sometimes externally, often internally, that what you have built is close to its natural limit.

It sounds like:

- This is probably as big as it gets.
- I have a good thing. I should not mess it up.
- Scaling is for other kinds of businesses.
- Maybe this is meant to stay a lifestyle company.

For women entrepreneurs who are not interested in outside investors or venture capital, this lie can feel especially convincing. Without the hype of funding rounds or splashy headlines, growth past seven figures can seem opaque, even inaccessible.

But here is the truth: **There is no ceiling.** There are only constraints that you're imposing on yourself. Most businesses do not stall because the founder lacks ambition or capability. They stall because the business model, systems, or leadership structure were designed for a smaller version of the company and never evolved.

What worked at two hundred thousand dollars in revenue will not work at one million. What worked at one million will not work at three. This is not failure. It is physics. Growth requires increased capacity. Capacity is created through systems, pricing, team structure, decision rights, and a shift in how the founder spends her time. None of these require outside capital. They require intention.

Many women are taught how to operate a business but not how to build one. They become indispensable to every function. They stay deeply involved in delivery, client management, problem-solving, and quality control. The business runs well because they are everywhere. And that is exactly what creates the illusion of a ceiling.

When you are the system, the business can only grow as far as you can stretch. The shift from operator to builder is where scaling actually happens. That shift often triggers discomfort. Letting go feels risky. Delegating feels inefficient at first. Designing systems feels slower than just doing the work yourself. But this is where leadership evolves.

Scaling is not about doing more. It is about doing differently. A business crosses the million-dollar mark when the founder stops asking, "How do I do this better?" and starts asking, "How does this get done without me at the center of it?"

That is not a loss of control. It is an expansion of impact. The lie of the ceiling keeps women playing defense. It frames growth as dangerous rather than strategic. It encourages preservation over evolution.

But businesses that do not evolve eventually stall, not because they grew too much, but because they did not redesign themselves in time.

You do not need permission to want more. You do not need a different personality, a different business, or a different market. You need to build the next version of your company on purpose.

The ceiling is not above you. It is behind you.

As you begin to dismantle the idea of a ceiling, another belief often rushes in to fill the gap. This one appeals to pride, independence, and identity. It tells you that doing it alone is a badge of honor. That asking for help means you are not capable enough to handle what you have built. This lie has kept more women exhausted and isolated than almost any other.

<center>~~~~~~~~~~~~~~~~~~~</center>

Choose Your Reframe

Even when you recognize a thought as a lie, it can be surprisingly hard to stop listening to it. Awareness alone is rarely enough. When your brain is under pressure, it will default to familiar patterns unless you give it something more useful to reach for. Creating an empowering reframe gives you an intentional response to use when the old narrative shows up.

Below are several possible reframes for this lie. Choose the one that feels most believable and supportive to practice the next time this lie appears. If it stops working, choose a different one.

- **Option A:** Growth slows when systems lag, not because ability runs out.
- **Option B:** There is no ceiling. There is only the next structure I need to build.
- **Option C:** Scaling is a design problem, not a personal limitation.

One Action to Take

Step back and document where you are still acting as the primary system in your business. Choose one of those areas where you can begin building structure, whether that is process documentation, a role definition, or a hiring plan for the next stage.

Reflection Questions to Journal About

1. Where do you sense hesitation or fear around growth in your business right now?
2. How much of your business currently depends on you being involved in everything?

3. Which systems or structures have not evolved
    alongside your revenue or demand?
4. What would it look like to design the next version of
    your business on purpose?

Lie #6: Asking for Help Means You Can't Hack It

This lie is deeply intertwined with how many women learn to survive. From an early age, competence is rewarded. Self-sufficiency is praised. Being the one who can handle everything becomes part of the identity. By the time a woman starts and grows a business, she is often very good at carrying weight quietly.

So when the business grows and the load increases, her instinct is not to ask for help. It is to carry more.

This lie shows up in subtle ways:

- I should be able to figure this out myself.
- I do not want to burden anyone.
- It is faster if I just do it.
- Once things settle down, then I will get support.

The problem is that things do not settle down. Growth increases complexity. More clients, more revenue, more decisions, more risk. The belief that you should handle all of that alone does not make you stronger. It makes you smaller.

No meaningful business is built in isolation. The entrepreneurs who scale successfully are not the most independent. They are the most supported. They build teams, advisors, peers, and systems around them that extend their capacity and challenge their blind spots.

Many women confuse help with dependency. But help is not weakness. It is leverage. Delegation is not an admission that you are failing. It is a recognition that your time and energy are better spent leading than managing every detail. Seeking advice is not uncertainty. It is strategic humility.

The reluctance to ask for help often has less to do with competence and more to do with control. When you have learned to rely only on yourself, trusting others feels risky. Letting go of tasks feels like letting go of identity.

But holding onto everything yourself has a cost. It limits growth. It narrows perspective. It reinforces the belief that you must earn rest through exhaustion.

Support does not dilute leadership. It amplifies it. When you allow others to contribute, you gain space to think, decide, and lead at a higher level. You also model a healthier form of leadership, one that values collaboration over martyrdom.

Asking for help is not a failure of capability. It is a commitment to sustainability. The strongest leaders are not the ones who carry everything alone. They are the ones who know which weight is theirs to carry and which weight should be shared.

When you release the need to do everything alone, one final lie often makes a last attempt to hold its ground. It frames success as a trade-off. It suggests that ambition and fulfillment cannot coexist. That building something meaningful requires sacrificing the rest of your life. This lie is so normalized that many women stop questioning it altogether.

<center>~~~~~~~~~~~~~~~~~</center>

Choose Your Reframe

Even when you recognize a thought as a lie, it can be surprisingly hard to stop listening to it. Awareness alone is rarely enough. When your brain is under pressure, it will default to familiar patterns unless you give it something more useful to reach for. Creating an empowering reframe gives you an intentional response to use when the old narrative shows up.

Below are several possible reframes for this lie. Choose the one that feels most believable and supportive to practice the next time this lie appears. If it stops working, choose a different one.

- **Option A:** Support expands my capacity and strengthens my leadership.
- **Option B:** Delegation is a strategic decision, not a personal failure.
- **Option C:** I lead best when I am supported, not isolated.

One Action to Take

Ask for support in one specific way this month. This could be delegating a task, seeking advice from a peer, or bringing in expertise you have been trying to replace with your own effort.

Reflection Questions to Journal About

1. What support have you been postponing or avoiding, and why?
2. What beliefs do you hold about independence that may no longer serve your business?
3. Which tasks or decisions would benefit most from being shared or delegated?
4. Who could be part of your support ecosystem over the next year?

Lie #7: Success Requires Choosing Between Your Business and Your Personal Life

This lie is persistent because it has been modeled for generations. We have been shown images of success that look singular and consuming. Long hours. Missed moments. Constant availability. The narrative says that if you want something extraordinary, you must give up everything else.

For women entrepreneurs, this lie is often layered with guilt: If you are working, you feel you should be more present elsewhere. If you are resting, you feel you should be doing more. If you want both achievement and enjoyment, you worry that means you are not serious enough.

So you compromise yourself. You postpone joy. You minimize needs. You tell yourself life will happen later. The problem is that later keeps moving.

This lie convinces women that fulfillment is something to be earned after success rather than something that sustains it. It frames personal life as a distraction instead of a source of strength.

But here is the truth: A depleted leader does not build a thriving business. Energy, creativity, perspective, and resilience do not come from constant output. They come from living a full life. Relationships, rest, interests, and joy are not competing priorities. They are inputs.

The idea of balance often misses the point. Balance implies constant trade-offs, as if time spent in one area must be stolen from another. A more useful model is integration. When your business is designed to support your life and your life supports your leadership, both become stronger.

This requires intention. It means designing work that aligns with your values rather than overrides them. It means making decisions based not only on revenue, but on sustainability. It means recognizing that success measured only by growth eventually hollowed out the person who achieved it.

Women do not need to choose between ambition and fulfillment. They need permission to define success on their own terms.

The lie that success requires sacrifice keeps women chasing someone else's version of achievement. Letting go of that lie allows you to build a business that reflects who you are, not who you were told to be.

You do not scale by abandoning yourself. You scale by bringing your whole self with you.

~~~~~~~~~~~~~~~~~~

Choose Your Reframe

Even when you recognize a thought as a lie, it can be surprisingly hard to stop listening to it. Awareness alone is rarely enough. When your brain is under pressure, it will default to familiar patterns unless you give it something more useful to reach for. Creating an empowering reframe gives you an intentional response to use when the old narrative shows up.
~~~~~~~~~~~~~~~~~~

Below are several possible reframes for this lie. Choose the one that feels most believable and supportive to practice the next time this lie appears. If it stops working, choose a different one.

- **Option A:** My life fuels my business. It is not in competition with it.
- **Option B:** Sustainable success is designed, not sacrificed for.
- **Option C:** I get to define success in a way that supports both growth and well-being.

One Action to Take:

Make one decision that protects both your business and your well-being. This might be setting a boundary, declining an opportunity that does not align, or intentionally scheduling something that restores your energy and creativity.

Reflection Questions to Journal About

1. How do you currently define success, and whose definition is it really?

2. Where are you sacrificing sustainability in the name of achievement?

3. What parts of your life most directly fuel your creativity and leadership?

4. What would an integrated version of success look like for you in this season?

Conclusion

By now, you have seen how these lies operate.

Not as dramatic moments of self-doubt, but as quiet assumptions that shape everyday decisions. How you price. How you speak. How you rest. How you grow. None of these lies appeared out of nowhere. They were heard, learned, reinforced, and repeated until they felt like facts.

But they were never facts. They were inherited narratives. Outdated expectations. Mental shortcuts your brain adopted to keep you safe.

The most important thing to understand is this: your brain was not trying to sabotage you. It was trying to protect you using old information. The problem is that protection eventually becomes limitation if it is never questioned.

Every lie we have dismantled in this book has one thing in common. It shrinks your range of motion:

- It keeps you waiting when you are ready.
- It keeps you undercharging when you are delivering real value.

- It keeps you exhausted when systems are needed.
- It keeps you quiet when clarity is required.
- It keeps you capped when growth is possible.
- It keeps you alone when support would accelerate everything.
- It keeps you sacrificing when integration would sustain you.

Uninstalling these lies does not happen all at once. It happens through awareness, repetition, and choice. Each time you notice the old narrative and respond differently, you rewrite the code your leadership runs on.

That is the real work. Leadership is not about eliminating fear or doubt. It is about learning which thoughts deserve authority and which ones do not. It is about trusting yourself enough to act before certainty arrives. It is about designing a business that reflects your values, not just your capacity for endurance.

You do not need to become someone else to lead bigger. You do not need to prove yourself worthy of more. You do not need permission to want what you want.

You are already capable of the next level. The work now is alignment. Between what you believe and how you lead. Between what you tolerate and what you are building. Between the voice you listen to most and the life you want to create.

This book is not a finish line. It is a reset. A reminder that you get to question the stories running in your head. You get to choose which ones stay. And you get to lead from a place of clarity, confidence, and self-trust rather than fear and conditioning.

The lies may still knock from time to time. Now you know not to answer the door.

Additional Resources

I created some additional resources to help you figure out where your brain's lies came from and to reinforce your reframes. Scan the code below to access them.

By the way, I readily admit that I used AI to help create and edit this book, as well as help me brainstorm the additional resources that would be most valuable for readers. But the message and concepts are all mine.

About Molly Gimmel

Molly Gimmel is a serial entrepreneur and leadership expert who understands firsthand the challenges women face while building and growing companies. As a past National Chair of the National Association of Women Business Owners (NAWBO), she has supported and advocated for women entrepreneurs nationwide and internationally. Through her writing, speaking, and work at Vellamo Leadership Institute, Molly helps women stop shrinking and start leading bigger, more sustainable businesses.

Connect with her on LinkedIn at:
http://linkedin.com/in/mollygimmel